- CHRISTMAS BEGINS WITH

Christ-Centered Christmas Planning for _____
YEAR

NOVEMBER
SUN	MON	TUE	WED	THU	FRI	SAT

DECEMBER
SUN	MON	TUE	WED	THU	FRI	SAT

JANUARY
SUN	MON	TUE	WED	THU	FRI	SAT

- CHRISTMAS MISSION STATEMENT -

This is what I want my Christ-Centered Christmas to look like...

Christmas Prayer

Bless us Lord this Christmas with
Peace that surpasses all understanding,
Joy that is beyond material possessions,
Love that knows no boundaries, and
Strength that emanates from
FAITH IN YOU.

- HOLIDAY PLANNER INDEX -

	CONTENTS	PAGE	✓
1	The Christmas Story as told by Luke	1-2	
2	The Christmas Story as told by Matthew	3-4	
3	Monthly Calendar for November	5-6	
4	Monthly Calendar for December	7-8	
5	Monthly Calendar for January	9-10	
6	12 Weekly Schedule Pages	11-34	
7	25 Days of Christmas Devotionals Planning	35	
8	25 Days of Christmas Giving Planning (Acts of Kindness & Service)	36	
9	Holiday Bucket List (25 Ways I can please the Savior)	37	
10	Holiday Bucket List (25 Meaningful things to do with family & friends)	38	
11	Holiday To Do List	39-42	
12	Holiday Budget Planner	43-44	
13	Holiday Gift List	45-46	
14	Holiday Priority Recipient Gift List	47-56	
15	Black Friday Shopping List	57-58	
16	Cyber Monday Shopping List	59-60	
17	Holiday Traditions	61	
18	Christ-Centered Christmas Tradition Ideas	62	
19	Scripture References for Hope, Love, Joy & Peace	63	
20	Christmas Related Bible Verses	64	
21	Holiday Music, Movies, Books, Activities & Games	65-68	
22	Holiday Menu Planner	69-78	
23	Holiday Recipes	79-98	
24	Decoration Inventory	99-100	
25	My Christmas Wishlist	101	
26	Gifts I Received & Gratitude	102	
27	My Vision Board for the New Year	103	
28	My New Year's Resolutions	104	
29	Christmas & New Year's Card List	105-110	
30	Extra Holiday Lined Note Pages	111-112	
31	Extra Holiday Bullet Dot Note Pages	113-114	
32	Extra Holiday Checklists	115-116	

THE CHRISTMAS STORY

The Story of the Birth of Christ As told through Luke
King James Version (KJV)

Luke 2:1 And it came to pass in those days, that there went out a decree from Caesar Augustus, that all the world should be taxed. 2:2 (And this taxing was first made when Cyrenius was governor of Syria.) 2:3 And all went to be taxed, every one into his own city. 2:4 And Joseph also went up from Galilee, out of the city of Nazareth, into Judaea, unto the city of David, which is called Bethlehem; (because he was of the house and lineage of David:) 2:5 To be taxed with Mary his espoused wife, being great with Child. 2:6 And so it was, that, while they were there, the days were accomplished that she should be delivered. 2:7 And she brought forth her firstborn Son, and wrapped Him in swaddling clothes, and laid Him in a manger; because there was no room for them in the inn. 2:8 And there were in the same country shepherds abiding in the field, keeping watch over their flock by night. 2:9 And, lo, the angel of the LORD came upon them, and the glory of the LORD shone round about them: and they were sore afraid. 2:10 And the angel said unto them, Fear not: for, behold, I bring you good tidings of great joy, which shall be to all people. 2:11 For unto you is born this day in the city of David a Saviour, which is Christ the LORD. 2:12 And this shall be a sign unto you; Ye shall find the Babe wrapped in swaddling clothes, lying in a manger. 2:13 And suddenly there was with the angel a multitude of the heavenly host praising God, and saying, 2:14 Glory to God in the highest, and on earth peace, good will toward men. 2:15 And it came to pass, as the angels were gone away from them into Heaven, the shepherds said one to another, Let us now go even unto Bethlehem, and see this thing which is come to pass, which the LORD hath made known unto us. 2:16 And they came with haste, and found Mary, and Joseph, and the Babe lying in a manger. 2:17 And when they had seen it, they made known abroad the saying which was told them concerning this Child. 2:18 And all they that heard it wondered at those things which were told them by the shepherds. 2:19 But Mary kept all these things, and pondered them in her heart. 2:20 And the shepherds returned, glorifying and praising God for all the things that they had heard and seen, as it was told unto them. 2:21 And when eight days were accomplished for the circumcising of the Child, His Name was called JESUS, which was so named of the angel before He was conceived in the womb.

THE CHRISTMAS STORY

The Story of the Birth of Christ As told through Matthew
King James Version (KJV)

Matthew 1:16 And Jacob begat Joseph the husband of Mary, of whom was born Jesus, Who is called Christ. 1:17 So all the generations from Abraham to David are fourteen generations; and from David until the carrying away into Babylon are fourteen generations; and from the carrying away into Babylon unto Christ are fourteen generations. 1:18 Now the birth of Jesus Christ was on this wise: When as His mother Mary was espoused to Joseph, before they came together, she was found with Child of the Holy Ghost. 1:19 Then Joseph her husband, being a just man, and not willing to make her a public example, was minded to put her away privily. 1:20 But while he thought on these things, behold, the angel of the LORD appeared unto him in a dream, saying, Joseph, thou son of David, fear not to take unto thee Mary thy wife: for That which is conceived in her is of the Holy Ghost. 1:21 And she shall bring forth a Son, and thou shalt call His Name JESUS: for He shall save His people from their sins. 1:22 Now all this was done, that it might be fulfilled which was spoken of the LORD by the prophet, saying, 1:23 Behold, a virgin shall be with Child, and shall bring forth a Son, and they shall call His Name Emmanuel, which being interpreted is, God With Us. 1:24 Then Joseph being raised from sleep did as the angel of the LORD had bidden him, and took unto him his wife: 1:25 And knew her not till she had brought forth her firstborn Son: and he called His Name JESUS. 2:1 Now when Jesus was born in Bethlehem of Judaea in the days of Herod the king, behold, there came wise men from the east to Jerusalem, 2:2 Saying, Where is He that is born King of the Jews? For we have seen His Star in the east, and are come to worship Him. 2:3 When Herod the king had heard these things, he was troubled, and all Jerusalem with him. 2:4 And when he had gathered all the chief priests and scribes of the people together, he demanded of them where Christ should be born. 2:5 And they said unto him, In Bethlehem of Judaea: for thus it is written by the prophet, 2:6 And thou Bethlehem, in the land of Juda, art not the least among the princes of Juda: for out of thee shall come a Governor, that shall rule My people Israel. 2:7 Then Herod, when he had privily called the wise men, inquired of them diligently what time the Star appeared. 2:8 And he sent them to Bethlehem, and said, Go and search diligently for the young Child; and when ye have found Him, bring me word again, that I may come and worship Him also. 2:9 When they had heard the king, they departed; and, lo, the Star, which they saw in the east, went before them, till it came and stood over where the young Child was. 2:10 When they saw the Star, they rejoiced with exceeding great joy. 2:11 And when they were come into the house, they saw the young Child with Mary His mother, and fell down, and worshipped Him: and when they had opened their treasures, they presented unto Him gifts; gold, and frankincense, and myrrh.

NOVEMBER

SUNDAY	MONDAY	TUESDAY	WEDNESDAY

Jesus is the light of our Christmas, the joy of our hearts and the hope of our world.

THURSDAY	FRIDAY	SATURDAY

Notes for the *MONTH*

DECEMBER

SUNDAY	MONDAY	TUESDAY	WEDNESDAY

Celebrate the miracle of this special season with joy, peace and the lord in your heart.

THURSDAY	FRIDAY	SATURDAY

Notes for the *MONTH*

JANUARY

SUNDAY	MONDAY	TUESDAY	WEDNESDAY

The most important part of CHRISTMAS is the first six letters!

THURSDAY	FRIDAY	SATURDAY

Notes for the MONTH

WEEKLY Schedule

DATE	SUNDAY	MONDAY	TUESDAY	WEDNESDAY
5:00				
5:30				
6:00				
6:30				
7:00				
7:30				
8:00				
8:30				
9:00				
9:30				
10:00				
10:30				
11:00				
11:30				
12:00				
12:30				
1:00				
1:30				
2:00				
2:30				
3:00				
3:30				
4:00				
4:30				
5:00				
5:30				
6:00				
6:30				
7:00				
7:30				
8:00				

For unto us a child is born, unto us a son is given. - Isaiah 9:6

DATE	THURSDAY	FRIDAY	SATURDAY	WEEKLY NOTES
5:00				
5:30				
6:00				
6:30				
7:00				
7:30				
8:00				
8:30				
9:00				
9:30				
10:00				
10:30				
11:00				
11:30				
12:00				
12:30				
1:00				
1:30				
2:00				
2:30				
3:00				
3:30				
4:00				
4:30				
5:00				
5:30				
6:00				
6:30				
7:00				
7:30				
8:00				

WEEKLY *Schedule*

	SUNDAY	MONDAY	TUESDAY	WEDNESDAY
DATE				
5:00				
5:30				
6:00				
6:30				
7:00				
7:30				
8:00				
8:30				
9:00				
9:30				
10:00				
10:30				
11:00				
11:30				
12:00				
12:30				
1:00				
1:30				
2:00				
2:30				
3:00				
3:30				
4:00				
4:30				
5:00				
5:30				
6:00				
6:30				
7:00				
7:30				
8:00				

Take time to thank HIM for the gift we received thousands of years ago.

DATE	THURSDAY	FRIDAY	SATURDAY	WEEKLY NOTES
5:00				
5:30				
6:00				
6:30				
7:00				
7:30				
8:00				
8:30				
9:00				
9:30				
10:00				
10:30				
11:00				
11:30				
12:00				
12:30				
1:00				
1:30				
2:00				
2:30				
3:00				
3:30				
4:00				
4:30				
5:00				
5:30				
6:00				
6:30				
7:00				
7:30				
8:00				

WEEKLY Schedule

	SUNDAY	MONDAY	TUESDAY	WEDNESDAY
DATE				
5:00				
5:30				
6:00				
6:30				
7:00				
7:30				
8:00				
8:30				
9:00				
9:30				
10:00				
10:30				
11:00				
11:30				
12:00				
12:30				
1:00				
1:30				
2:00				
2:30				
3:00				
3:30				
4:00				
4:30				
5:00				
5:30				
6:00				
6:30				
7:00				
7:30				
8:00				

Let the true light of Christmas shine bright through you.

DATE	THURSDAY	FRIDAY	SATURDAY	WEEKLY NOTES
5:00				
5:30				
6:00				
6:30				
7:00				
7:30				
8:00				
8:30				
9:00				
9:30				
10:00				
10:30				
11:00				
11:30				
12:00				
12:30				
1:00				
1:30				
2:00				
2:30				
3:00				
3:30				
4:00				
4:30				
5:00				
5:30				
6:00				
6:30				
7:00				
7:30				
8:00				

WEEKLY *Schedule*

	SUNDAY	MONDAY	TUESDAY	WEDNESDAY
DATE				
5:00				
5:30				
6:00				
6:30				
7:00				
7:30				
8:00				
8:30				
9:00				
9:30				
10:00				
10:30				
11:00				
11:30				
12:00				
12:30				
1:00				
1:30				
2:00				
2:30				
3:00				
3:30				
4:00				
4:30				
5:00				
5:30				
6:00				
6:30				
7:00				
7:30				
8:00				

Thanks be to God for his indescribable gift! - 2 Corinthians 9:15

DATE	THURSDAY	FRIDAY	SATURDAY	WEEKLY NOTES
5:00				
5:30				
6:00				
6:30				
7:00				
7:30				
8:00				
8:30				
9:00				
9:30				
10:00				
10:30				
11:00				
11:30				
12:00				
12:30				
1:00				
1:30				
2:00				
2:30				
3:00				
3:30				
4:00				
4:30				
5:00				
5:30				
6:00				
6:30				
7:00				
7:30				
8:00				

WEEKLY *Schedule*

	SUNDAY	MONDAY	TUESDAY	WEDNESDAY
DATE				
5:00				
5:30				
6:00				
6:30				
7:00				
7:30				
8:00				
8:30				
9:00				
9:30				
10:00				
10:30				
11:00				
11:30				
12:00				
12:30				
1:00				
1:30				
2:00				
2:30				
3:00				
3:30				
4:00				
4:30				
5:00				
5:30				
6:00				
6:30				
7:00				
7:30				
8:00				

Rejoice the spirit of Christmas with friends, family & Christ!

DATE	THURSDAY	FRIDAY	SATURDAY	WEEKLY NOTES
5:00				
5:30				
6:00				
6:30				
7:00				
7:30				
8:00				
8:30				
9:00				
9:30				
10:00				
10:30				
11:00				
11:30				
12:00				
12:30				
1:00				
1:30				
2:00				
2:30				
3:00				
3:30				
4:00				
4:30				
5:00				
5:30				
6:00				
6:30				
7:00				
7:30				
8:00				

WEEKLY *Schedule*

	SUNDAY	MONDAY	TUESDAY	WEDNESDAY
DATE				
5:00				
5:30				
6:00				
6:30				
7:00				
7:30				
8:00				
8:30				
9:00				
9:30				
10:00				
10:30				
11:00				
11:30				
12:00				
12:30				
1:00				
1:30				
2:00				
2:30				
3:00				
3:30				
4:00				
4:30				
5:00				
5:30				
6:00				
6:30				
7:00				
7:30				
8:00				

May the love of our Savior, Jesus Christ, be with you always.

DATE	THURSDAY	FRIDAY	SATURDAY	WEEKLY NOTES
5:00				
5:30				
6:00				
6:30				
7:00				
7:30				
8:00				
8:30				
9:00				
9:30				
10:00				
10:30				
11:00				
11:30				
12:00				
12:30				
1:00				
1:30				
2:00				
2:30				
3:00				
3:30				
4:00				
4:30				
5:00				
5:30				
6:00				
6:30				
7:00				
7:30				
8:00				

WEEKLY Schedule

	SUNDAY	MONDAY	TUESDAY	WEDNESDAY
DATE				
5:00				
5:30				
6:00				
6:30				
7:00				
7:30				
8:00				
8:30				
9:00				
9:30				
10:00				
10:30				
11:00				
11:30				
12:00				
12:30				
1:00				
1:30				
2:00				
2:30				
3:00				
3:30				
4:00				
4:30				
5:00				
5:30				
6:00				
6:30				
7:00				
7:30				
8:00				

In the darkest nights, Christ's love still shines the brightest!

DATE	THURSDAY	FRIDAY	SATURDAY	WEEKLY NOTES
5:00				
5:30				
6:00				
6:30				
7:00				
7:30				
8:00				
8:30				
9:00				
9:30				
10:00				
10:30				
11:00				
11:30				
12:00				
12:30				
1:00				
1:30				
2:00				
2:30				
3:00				
3:30				
4:00				
4:30				
5:00				
5:30				
6:00				
6:30				
7:00				
7:30				
8:00				

WEEKLY *Schedule*

DATE	SUNDAY	MONDAY	TUESDAY	WEDNESDAY
5:00				
5:30				
6:00				
6:30				
7:00				
7:30				
8:00				
8:30				
9:00				
9:30				
10:00				
10:30				
11:00				
11:30				
12:00				
12:30				
1:00				
1:30				
2:00				
2:30				
3:00				
3:30				
4:00				
4:30				
5:00				
5:30				
6:00				
6:30				
7:00				
7:30				
8:00				

The essence of Christmas is not in the presents but in Christ!

DATE	THURSDAY	FRIDAY	SATURDAY	WEEKLY NOTES
5:00				
5:30				
6:00				
6:30				
7:00				
7:30				
8:00				
8:30				
9:00				
9:30				
10:00				
10:30				
11:00				
11:30				
12:00				
12:30				
1:00				
1:30				
2:00				
2:30				
3:00				
3:30				
4:00				
4:30				
5:00				
5:30				
6:00				
6:30				
7:00				
7:30				
8:00				

WEEKLY Schedule

	SUNDAY	MONDAY	TUESDAY	WEDNESDAY
DATE				
5:00				
5:30				
6:00				
6:30				
7:00				
7:30				
8:00				
8:30				
9:00				
9:30				
10:00				
10:30				
11:00				
11:30				
12:00				
12:30				
1:00				
1:30				
2:00				
2:30				
3:00				
3:30				
4:00				
4:30				
5:00				
5:30				
6:00				
6:30				
7:00				
7:30				
8:00				

Wake up today and start your day with heartfelt thanks for the birth of our Savior.

DATE	THURSDAY	FRIDAY	SATURDAY	WEEKLY NOTES
5:00				
5:30				
6:00				
6:30				
7:00				
7:30				
8:00				
8:30				
9:00				
9:30				
10:00				
10:30				
11:00				
11:30				
12:00				
12:30				
1:00				
1:30				
2:00				
2:30				
3:00				
3:30				
4:00				
4:30				
5:00				
5:30				
6:00				
6:30				
7:00				
7:30				
8:00				

WEEKLY *Schedule*

	SUNDAY	MONDAY	TUESDAY	WEDNESDAY
DATE				
5:00				
5:30				
6:00				
6:30				
7:00				
7:30				
8:00				
8:30				
9:00				
9:30				
10:00				
10:30				
11:00				
11:30				
12:00				
12:30				
1:00				
1:30				
2:00				
2:30				
3:00				
3:30				
4:00				
4:30				
5:00				
5:30				
6:00				
6:30				
7:00				
7:30				
8:00				

Wishing you have a BLESSED Christmas & Happy New Year!

DATE	THURSDAY	FRIDAY	SATURDAY	WEEKLY NOTES
5:00				
5:30				
6:00				
6:30				
7:00				
7:30				
8:00				
8:30				
9:00				
9:30				
10:00				
10:30				
11:00				
11:30				
12:00				
12:30				
1:00				
1:30				
2:00				
2:30				
3:00				
3:30				
4:00				
4:30				
5:00				
5:30				
6:00				
6:30				
7:00				
7:30				
8:00				

WEEKLY *Schedule*

	SUNDAY	MONDAY	TUESDAY	WEDNESDAY
DATE				
5:00				
5:30				
6:00				
6:30				
7:00				
7:30				
8:00				
8:30				
9:00				
9:30				
10:00				
10:30				
11:00				
11:30				
12:00				
12:30				
1:00				
1:30				
2:00				
2:30				
3:00				
3:30				
4:00				
4:30				
5:00				
5:30				
6:00				
6:30				
7:00				
7:30				
8:00				

May you find peace in God & warmth in the Light of Christ!

DATE	THURSDAY	FRIDAY	SATURDAY	WEEKLY NOTES
5:00				
5:30				
6:00				
6:30				
7:00				
7:30				
8:00				
8:30				
9:00				
9:30				
10:00				
10:30				
11:00				
11:30				
12:00				
12:30				
1:00				
1:30				
2:00				
2:30				
3:00				
3:30				
4:00				
4:30				
5:00				
5:30				
6:00				
6:30				
7:00				
7:30				
8:00				

WEEKLY *Schedule*

	SUNDAY	MONDAY	TUESDAY	WEDNESDAY
DATE				
5:00				
5:30				
6:00				
6:30				
7:00				
7:30				
8:00				
8:30				
9:00				
9:30				
10:00				
10:30				
11:00				
11:30				
12:00				
12:30				
1:00				
1:30				
2:00				
2:30				
3:00				
3:30				
4:00				
4:30				
5:00				
5:30				
6:00				
6:30				
7:00				
7:30				
8:00				

Love, Joy and Peace: Today, Tomorrow and Always!

DATE	THURSDAY	FRIDAY	SATURDAY	WEEKLY NOTES
5:00				
5:30				
6:00				
6:30				
7:00				
7:30				
8:00				
8:30				
9:00				
9:30				
10:00				
10:30				
11:00				
11:30				
12:00				
12:30				
1:00				
1:30				
2:00				
2:30				
3:00				
3:30				
4:00				
4:30				
5:00				
5:30				
6:00				
6:30				
7:00				
7:30				
8:00				

- 25 DAYS OF CHRISTMAS DEVOTIONALS -

#	DEVOTIONAL LESSON/CONCEPT TO STUDY	BOOK/CHAPTER/VERSE	✓
1			
2			
3			
4			
5			
6			
7			
8			
9			
10			
11			
12			
13			
14			
15			
16			
17			
18			
19			
20			
21			
22			
23			
24			
25			

- 25 DAYS OF CHRISTMAS GIVING -

#	CHRISTMAS ACTS OF KINDNESS & SERVICE	COMPLETED ON	✓
1			
2			
3			
4			
5			
6			
7			
8			
9			
10			
11			
12			
13			
14			
15			
16			
17			
18			
19			
20			
21			
22			
23			
24			
25			

- HOLIDAY BUCKET LIST -

#	WAYS I CAN PLEASE THE SAVIOR	COMPLETED ON	✓
1			
2			
3			
4			
5			
6			
7			
8			
9			
10			
11			
12			
13			
14			
15			
16			
17			
18			
19			
20			
21			
22			
23			
24			
25			

- HOLIDAY BUCKET LIST -

#	MEANINGFUL THINGS TO DO WITH FAMILY & FRIENDS	COMPLETED ON	✓
1			
2			
3			
4			
5			
6			
7			
8			
9			
10			
11			
12			
13			
14			
15			
16			
17			
18			
19			
20			
21			
22			
23			
24			
25			

- HOLIDAY TO-DO LIST -

#	TASK/PROJECTS/EVENTS	COMPLETE BY	✓
1			
2			
3			
4			
5			
6			
7			
8			
9			
10			
11			
12			
13			
14			
15			
16			
17			
18			
19			
20			
21			
22			
23			
24			
25			

- HOLIDAY TO-DO LIST -

#	TASK/PROJECTS/EVENTS	COMPLETE BY	✓
26			
27			
28			
29			
30			
31			
32			
33			
34			
35			
36			
37			
38			
39			
40			
41			
42			
43			
44			
45			
46			
47			
48			
49			
50			

- HOLIDAY TO-DO LIST -

#	TASK/PROJECTS/EVENTS	COMPLETE BY	✓
51			
52			
53			
54			
55			
56			
57			
58			
59			
60			
61			
62			
63			
64			
65			
66			
67			
68			
69			
70			
71			
72			
73			
74			
75			

- HOLIDAY TO-DO LIST -

#	TASK/PROJECTS/EVENTS	COMPLETE BY	✓
76			
77			
78			
79			
80			
81			
82			
83			
84			
85			
86			
87			
88			
89			
90			
91			
92			
93			
94			
95			
96			
97			
98			
99			
100			

- HOLIDAY BUDGET -

OVERVIEW

Planned Budget for the Holidays	
Actual Amount Spent	
Difference (Over or Under Budget)	

GIFTS	BUDGET	SPENT	DIFFERENCE
Immediate Family Members			
Stocking Stuffers			
Extended Family Members			
Friends			
Co-workers			
Neighbors			
Hostess Gifts			
Service Providers (Teachers, Mail Carrier, Cleaner etc.)			
Charity Gift Donations			
Emergency Generic Gifts (For people you forgot)			
Other:			
TOTAL			

PACKAGING & DELIVERY	BUDGET	SPENT	DIFFERENCE
Gift Wrapping			
Tags & Greeting Cards			
Boxes & Gift Bags			
Supplies (Ribbon, Tape, Glue, Scissors etc.)			
Postage			
Other:			
TOTAL			

TRAVEL	BUDGET	SPENT	DIFFERENCE
Airfare			
Lodging			
Transportation			
Pet Boarding/Sitter/Walker etc.			
Other:			
TOTAL			

ENTERTAINMENT	BUDGET	SPENT	DIFFERENCE
Eating Out			
Food & Beverages			
Tickets			
Special Events			
Other:			
TOTAL			

- HOLIDAY BUDGET -

HOLIDAY MEALS	BUDGET	SPENT	DIFFERENCE
Groceries for Breakfast			
Groceries for Lunch			
Groceries for Dinner			
Groceries for Special Dishes to take to Parties			
Other Groceries			
Pastries, Desserts & Snacks			
Beverages			
Meal Gift Donations			
Other:			
TOTAL			

MISCELLANEOUS	BUDGET	SPENT	DIFFERENCE
Disposables (Plates, Cups, Cutlery, Napkins etc.)			
Decorations (Tree, Lights, Ornaments, Nativity Set etc.)			
Floral Arrangements/Plants/Wreaths			
Clothing & Accessories			
Grooming (Hair, Nails, Makeup etc.)			
Photos			
Acts of Kindness & Service			
Monetary Donations			
Extra Utility Costs for Increase in Holiday Usage			
TOTAL			

UNPLANNED EXPENSES	COST
TOTAL	

UNEXPECTED BONUSES/ SAVINGS & REFUNDS	SAVINGS
TOTAL	

- HOLIDAY GIFT LIST -

✓	GIFT FOR	RELATION	# OF GIFTS	GIFT IDEAS	STORE
	TOTAL				

- HOLIDAY GIFT LIST -

	BLACK FRIDAY	CYBER MONDAY	CARD	WRAPPED	MAILED	RECEIVED	BUDGET	SPENT	COMMENTS (Order #, Tracking #, Notes etc.)

- HOLIDAY PRIORITY GIFT RECIPIENT -

Name _____

GOT GIFTS	WRAPPED	CARDED	DELIVERED	RECEIVED

BUDGET:

RECIPIENT'S WISHLIST	PRICE	✓
1		
2		
3		

OTHER GIFT IDEAS

1		
2		
3		

MY ACTS OF KINDNESS FOR YOU

1.
2.
3.

MY ACTS OF SERVICE FOR YOU

1.
2.
3.

SCRIPTURES *to strengthen our relationship*

MY CHRISTMAS PRAYER FOR YOU

NOTES:

TOTAL SPENT:

- HOLIDAY PRIORITY GIFT RECIPIENT -

48

Name _____

	GOT GIFTS	WRAPPED	CARDED	DELIVERED	RECEIVED

BUDGET:

RECIPIENT'S WISHLIST	PRICE	✓
1		
2		
3		

OTHER GIFT IDEAS

1		
2		
3		

MY ACTS OF KINDNESS FOR YOU

1.
2.
3.

MY ACTS OF SERVICE FOR YOU

1.
2.
3.

SCRIPTURES *to strengthen our relationship*

MY CHRISTMAS PRAYER FOR YOU

NOTES:

TOTAL SPENT:

- HOLIDAY PRIORITY GIFT RECIPIENT -

Name _____

GOT GIFTS | WRAPPED | CARDED | DELIVERED | RECEIVED

BUDGET:

RECIPIENT'S WISHLIST	PRICE	✓
1		
2		
3		

OTHER GIFT IDEAS

1		
2		
3		

MY ACTS OF KINDNESS FOR YOU

1		
2		
3		

MY ACTS OF SERVICE FOR YOU

1		
2		
3		

SCRIPTURES *to strengthen our relationship*

MY CHRISTMAS PRAYER FOR YOU

NOTES:

TOTAL SPENT:

- HOLIDAY PRIORITY GIFT RECIPIENT -

Name _____

	GOT GIFTS	WRAPPED	CARDED	DELIVERED	RECEIVED

BUDGET:

RECIPIENT'S WISHLIST	PRICE	✓
1		
2		
3		

OTHER GIFT IDEAS

1		
2		
3		

MY ACTS OF KINDNESS FOR YOU

1	
2	
3	

MY ACTS OF SERVICE FOR YOU

1	
2	
3	

SCRIPTURES *to strengthen our relationship*

MY CHRISTMAS PRAYER FOR YOU

NOTES:

TOTAL SPENT:

- HOLIDAY PRIORITY GIFT RECIPIENT -

Name _____

GOT GIFTS	WRAPPED	CARDED	DELIVERED	RECEIVED

BUDGET:

RECIPIENT'S WISHLIST	PRICE	✓
1		
2		
3		

OTHER GIFT IDEAS

1		
2		
3		

MY ACTS OF KINDNESS FOR YOU

1.
2.
3.

MY ACTS OF SERVICE FOR YOU

1.
2.
3.

SCRIPTURES *to strengthen our relationship*

MY CHRISTMAS PRAYER FOR YOU

NOTES:

TOTAL SPENT:

- HOLIDAY PRIORITY GIFT RECIPIENT -

Name _____

	GOT GIFTS	WRAPPED	CARDED	DELIVERED	RECEIVED

BUDGET:

RECIPIENT'S WISHLIST	PRICE	✓
1		
2		
3		

SCRIPTURES *to strengthen our relationship*

OTHER GIFT IDEAS

1		
2		
3		

MY ACTS OF KINDNESS FOR YOU

1
2
3

MY ACTS OF SERVICE FOR YOU

1
2
3

MY CHRISTMAS PRAYER FOR YOU

NOTES:

TOTAL SPENT:

- HOLIDAY PRIORITY GIFT RECIPIENT -

Name _____

GOT GIFTS	WRAPPED	CARDED	DELIVERED	RECEIVED

BUDGET:

RECIPIENT'S WISHLIST	**PRICE**	✓
1		
2		
3		

OTHER GIFT IDEAS

1		
2		
3		

MY ACTS OF KINDNESS FOR YOU

1
2
3

MY ACTS OF SERVICE FOR YOU

1
2
3

SCRIPTURES *to strengthen our relationship*

MY CHRISTMAS PRAYER FOR YOU

NOTES:

TOTAL SPENT:

- HOLIDAY PRIORITY GIFT RECIPIENT -

Name _____

	GOT GIFTS	WRAPPED	CARDED	DELIVERED	RECEIVED

BUDGET:

RECIPIENT'S WISHLIST	PRICE	✓
1		
2		
3		

OTHER GIFT IDEAS

1		
2		
3		

MY ACTS OF KINDNESS FOR YOU

1		
2		
3		

MY ACTS OF SERVICE FOR YOU

1		
2		
3		

SCRIPTURES *to strengthen our relationship*

MY CHRISTMAS PRAYER FOR YOU

NOTES:

TOTAL SPENT:

- HOLIDAY PRIORITY GIFT RECIPIENT -

Name _____

	GOT GIFTS	WRAPPED	CARDED	DELIVERED	RECEIVED

BUDGET:

RECIPIENT'S WISHLIST	PRICE	✓
1		
2		
3		

OTHER GIFT IDEAS

1		
2		
3		

MY ACTS OF KINDNESS FOR YOU

1	
2	
3	

MY ACTS OF SERVICE FOR YOU

1	
2	
3	

SCRIPTURES *to strengthen our relationship*

MY CHRISTMAS PRAYER FOR YOU

NOTES:

TOTAL SPENT:

- HOLIDAY PRIORITY GIFT RECIPIENT -

Name _____

	GOT GIFTS	WRAPPED	CARDED	DELIVERED	RECEIVED

BUDGET:

RECIPIENT'S WISHLIST	PRICE	✓
1		
2		
3		

OTHER GIFT IDEAS

1		
2		
3		

MY ACTS OF KINDNESS FOR YOU

1.
2.
3.

MY ACTS OF SERVICE FOR YOU

1.
2.
3.

SCRIPTURES *to strengthen our relationship*

MY CHRISTMAS PRAYER FOR YOU

NOTES:

TOTAL SPENT:

- BLACK FRIDAY SHOPPING LIST -

✓	STORE	DOORBUSTER TIME	ITEM(S)
	TOTAL		

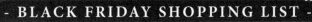

- BLACK FRIDAY SHOPPING LIST -

REGULAR PRICE	SALE PRICE	QUANTITY	BUDGET	SPENT	COMMENTS (Coupon Code, Rebates, Notes etc.)

- CYBER MONDAY SHOPPING LIST -

✓	WEBSITE	DELIVERY DATE	ITEM(S)
	TOTAL		

- CYBER MONDAY SHOPPING LIST -

	REGULAR PRICE	SALE PRICE	QUANTITY	BUDGET	SPENT	COMMENTS (Coupon Code, Tracking #, Notes etc.)

- HOLIDAY TRADITIONS -

Yearly Family Traditions

New Traditions to Add this Year

- CHRISTIAN CHRISTMAS TRADITION IDEAS -

- ☐ Read The Christmas Story from the Bible (Luke 2:1-21, Matthew 1:16-2:11)
- ☐ Attend a special Christmas church service
- ☐ Go Christmas Caroling
- ☐ Give a gift to a family in need
- ☐ Volunteer at a homeless shelter
- ☐ Observe & Celebrate Advent with calendars, Scripture readings & Devotionals
- ☐ Watch a Christian Christmas movie
- ☐ Visit a Live Nativity or Display your own Nativity Scene
- ☐ Read a Christ-Centered Christmas Storybook
- ☐ Have a Birthday Party for Jesus
- ☐ Write a Christmas letter to the Savior
- ☐ Put up a "Jesus Stocking" with letters of gratitude, prayers, gifts to donate etc.
- ☐ Give a thank you note in the mailboxes of those homes who display a Nativity
- ☐ Perform acts of service for those in need as well as family, friends and neighbors!
- ☐ Create or display your Jesse Tree (Isaiah 11:1-2)
- ☐ Decorate your home with Christ-Centered Decor
- ☐ Perform some Random Acts of Christmas Kindness
- ☐ Write out your Mission Statement for this Holiday Season
- ☐ Take some time to write out 3 Christ-Related promises to Jesus as a special gift
- ☐ Send out Christmas Cards that share a spiritual message
- ☐ Fill a Christmas Eve Box with fun activities and/or meaningful things to share
- ☐ Bake some Christmas cookies to share with your church
- ☐ Gather with your family and talk about the blessings God has given this year
- ☐ Make a gift or meal for your Pastor
- ☐ Take some quiet time for self-reflection and prayer

- CHRISTIAN SCRIPTURES -

For Hope	*For Love*	*For Joy*	*For Peace*
Isaiah 61:1-2	Isaiah 49:13-16	Isaiah 12:2-6	Isaiah 11:1-4
Jacob 4:4-5	1 Nephi 11:14-22	Isaiah 61:10	Isaiah 6-10
Romans 5:1-5	John 3:16-17	Mosiah 3:3-4	Isaiah 26:3-12
Romans 15:13	John 4:9-12	John 15:11	Isaiah 32:17
Romans 15:4	John 13:34-35	John 16:20-22	Isaiah 52:7
Hebrews 6:18-19	John 15:9-10	John 16:24	Isaiah 54:10
Hebrews 6:19	John 15:12-13	2 John 1:12	Isaiah 55:12
Hebrews 10:23	1 John 3:1	3 John 1:4	Leviticus 26:6
Hebrews 11:1	1 John 3:16-18	James 1:2-3	Luke 1:79
Deuteronomy 31-6	1 John 4:7-8	Psalm 16:11	Mark 4:39
1 Peter 1:13	1 John 4:11-12	Psalm 30:5	Matthew 11:28-30
1 Peter 1:3	1 John 4:16-18	Psalm 47:1	Mosiah 15:18-20
1 Peter 3:15	1 John 4:19	Psalm 94:19	Numbers 6:26
Psalm 9:18	1 John 4:20-21	Psalm 118:24	James 3:18
Psalm 42:11	Mark 12:29-31	Psalm 119:14	Jeremiah 29:11
Psalm 33:18	Moroni 7:47-48	Psalm 119:111	Jeremiah 33:6
Psalm 33:22	Colossians 3:14	Ecclesiastes 3:12-13	John 14:27
Psalm 39:7	1 Corinthians 13:1-5	Ecclesiastes 5:19	John 16:33
Psalm 71:5	1 Corinthians 13:13	Ecclesiastes 7:14	Philippians 4:6-7
Psalm 43:5	1 Corinthians 13:4-8	Ecclesiastes 9:7	Proverbs 3:2
Psalm 119:114	1 Corinthians 16:14	1 Peter 1:8-9	Proverbs 16:7
Psalm 130:5	1 Peter 4:8	Proverbs 10:28	Galatians 5:22-23
Proverbs 23:18	Proverbs 3:3-4	Proverbs 15:23	Hebrews 12:14
Proverbs 24:14	Proverbs 10:12	Proverbs 17:22	1 Peter 3:9-11
1 Thessalonians 4:16	Proverbs 17:17	Proverbs 23:24	1 Peter 5:7
1 Timothy 6:17	Proverbs 20:6-7	Philippians 1:25	Psalm 4:8
Titus 1:1-2	Romans 5:8	Philippians 4:4	Psalm 29:11
Matthew 11:28	Romans 12:9-10	Romans 5:3-4	Psalm 34:14
Mark 9:23	Romans 12:20-21	Romans 12:12	Psalm 37:11
Micah 7:7	Romans 13:8	Romans 12:15	Psalm 37:37
Moroni 7:41	Romans 13:10	Romans 14:17	Psalm 55:18
Job 5:15-16	Ephesians 2:4-5	Romans 15:13	Psalm 85:8
Job 11:18	Ephesians 4:2-3	Romans 15:32	Psalm 85:10
Jeremiah 29:11	Deuteronomy 7:9	Luke 15:7	Psalm 119:165
Luke 1:5-17	Luke 6:27-31	Nehemiah 8:10	Romans 12:17-21
1 Corinthians 15:19	Luke 6:35	Xephaniah 3:17	Romans 14:19
2 Corinthians 3:12-14	Matthew 5:43-48	Habakkuk 3:17-18	1 Thessalonians 3:16
Colossians 1:27	Philemon 1:7	2 Corinthians 6:10	1 Thessalonians 5:15
Ephesians 1:18	1 Thessalonians 3:12	1 Timothy 6:17	1 Corinthians 14:33

- CHRISTMAS BIBLE VERSES -

The Birth of Jesus

- [ ] Matthew 1:18-25
- [ ] Luke 2:1-14

The Visit of the Shepherds

- [ ] Luke 2:15-20

The Visit of the Magi (Wise Men)

- [ ] Matthew 2:1-12

Peace on Earth

- [ ] Luke 2:14

Immanuel

- [ ] Isaiah 7:14
- [ ] Matthew 1:23

The Gift of Eternal Life

- [ ] 1 John 5:11
- [ ] Romans 6:23
- [ ] John 3:16
- [ ] Titus 3:4-7
- [ ] John 10:27-28
- [ ] 1 Timothy 1:15-17

The Birth of Jesus Foretold

- [ ] Isaiah 40:1-11
- [ ] Luke 1:26-38

Mary's Song

- [ ] Luke 1:46-55

Powerful Christmas Verses

For God so loved the world that he gave his one and only Son, that whoever believes in him shall not perish but have eternal life.
- *John 3:16*

Thanks be to God for his indesribable gift!
- *2 Corinthians 9:15*

For to us a child is born, to us a son is given, and the government will be on his shoulders. And he will be called Wonderful Counselor, Mighty God, Everlasting Father, Prince of Peace.
- *Isaiah 9:6*

And this is the testimoney: God has given us eternal life, and this life is in his Son.
- *1 John 5:11*

And she shall bring forth a son, and thou shalt call his name Jesus: for he shall save his people from their sins.
- *Matthew 1:21*

A Merry Heart does good like medicine.
- *Proverbs 17:22*

When they saw the star, they rejoiced with exceeding great joy.
- *Matthew 2:10*

And the Word became flesh, and dwelt among us, and we saw His glory, glory as of the only begotten from the Father, full of grace and truth
- *John 1:14*

- HOLIDAY SONGS, MOVIES, BOOKS & ACTIVITIES/GAMES -

Title _____

FOR KIDS | FOR FAMILY | FOR ADULTS | FOR ALL | FOR ME

☐ Song ☐ Movie ☐ Book ☐ Activity/Game ☐ Other

DETAILS:

Title _____

FOR KIDS | FOR FAMILY | FOR ADULTS | FOR ALL | FOR ME

☐ Song ☐ Movie ☐ Book ☐ Activity/Game ☐ Other

DETAILS:

Title _____

FOR KIDS | FOR FAMILY | FOR ADULTS | FOR ALL | FOR ME

☐ Song ☐ Movie ☐ Book ☐ Activity/Game ☐ Other

DETAILS:

Title _____

FOR KIDS | FOR FAMILY | FOR ADULTS | FOR ALL | FOR ME

☐ Song ☐ Movie ☐ Book ☐ Activity/Game ☐ Other

DETAILS:

- HOLIDAY SONGS, MOVIES, BOOKS & ACTIVITIES/GAMES -

Title _____

	FOR KIDS	FOR FAMILY	FOR ADULTS	FOR ALL	FOR ME

☐ Song ☐ Movie ☐ Book ☐ Activity/Game ☐ Other

DETAILS:

Title _____

	FOR KIDS	FOR FAMILY	FOR ADULTS	FOR ALL	FOR ME

☐ Song ☐ Movie ☐ Book ☐ Activity/Game ☐ Other

DETAILS:

Title _____

	FOR KIDS	FOR FAMILY	FOR ADULTS	FOR ALL	FOR ME

☐ Song ☐ Movie ☐ Book ☐ Activity/Game ☐ Other

DETAILS:

Title _____

	FOR KIDS	FOR FAMILY	FOR ADULTS	FOR ALL	FOR ME

☐ Song ☐ Movie ☐ Book ☐ Activity/Game ☐ Other

DETAILS:

- HOLIDAY SONGS, MOVIES, BOOKS & ACTIVITIES/GAMES -

Title _____ FOR KIDS FOR FAMILY FOR ADULTS FOR ALL FOR ME

☐ Song ☐ Movie ☐ Book ☐ Activity/Game ☐ Other

DETAILS:

Title _____ FOR KIDS FOR FAMILY FOR ADULTS FOR ALL FOR ME

☐ Song ☐ Movie ☐ Book ☐ Activity/Game ☐ Other

DETAILS:

Title _____ FOR KIDS FOR FAMILY FOR ADULTS FOR ALL FOR ME

☐ Song ☐ Movie ☐ Book ☐ Activity/Game ☐ Other

DETAILS:

Title _____ FOR KIDS FOR FAMILY FOR ADULTS FOR ALL FOR ME

☐ Song ☐ Movie ☐ Book ☐ Activity/Game ☐ Other

DETAILS:

- HOLIDAY SONGS, MOVIES, BOOKS & ACTIVITIES/GAMES -

Title _____ FOR KIDS · FOR FAMILY · FOR ADULTS · FOR ALL · FOR ME

☐ Song ☐ Movie ☐ Book ☐ Activity/Game ☐ Other

DETAILS:

Title _____ FOR KIDS · FOR FAMILY · FOR ADULTS · FOR ALL · FOR ME

☐ Song ☐ Movie ☐ Book ☐ Activity/Game ☐ Other

DETAILS:

Title _____ FOR KIDS · FOR FAMILY · FOR ADULTS · FOR ALL · FOR ME

☐ Song ☐ Movie ☐ Book ☐ Activity/Game ☐ Other

DETAILS:

Popular Christian Christmas Suggestions

SONGS:
- Adore Him (Kari Jobe)
- Away in a Manger (James R. Murray)
- Joy to the World (Isaac Watts)
- Silent Night (Joseph Mohr & Franz Gruber)

BOOKS:
- God Gave Us Christmas (Lisa Bergren & David Hohn)
- The Christmas Story (Jane Watson & Eloise Wilkin)

MOVIES:
- The Nativity Story
- A Charlie Brown Christmas
- The Star of Bethlehem
- The Christmas Miracle

- Because of Bethlehem (Max Lucado)
- Baby Blessings Christmas (Alice Davidson)

- HOLIDAY MENU -

Date _____

STOCKED | PREPPED | MADE AHEAD | DELEGATED | DONE

BUDGET:	SPENT:		
BREAKFAST MENU		# OF GUESTS	**GROCERY LIST**
- Protein -	- Carbs/Grains -		
- Fruit & Veggies -	- Other -		
LUNCH MENU		# OF GUESTS	
- Appetizer -	- Side Dishes -		
- Main -	- Dessert -		
			TO DO LIST
DINNER MENU		# OF GUESTS	
- Appetizer -	- Side Dishes -		
- Main -	- Dessert -		
SNACKS	**DRINKS**		

NOTES:

- HOLIDAY MENU -

Date _____

STOCKED | PREPPED | MADE AHEAD | DELEGATED | DONE

BUDGET:	SPENT:

BREAKFAST MENU — # OF GUESTS

- Protein -	- Carbs/Grains -
- Fruit & Veggies -	- Other -

LUNCH MENU — # OF GUESTS

- Appetizer -	- Side Dishes -
- Main -	- Dessert -

DINNER MENU — # OF GUESTS

- Appetizer -	- Side Dishes -
- Main -	- Dessert -

SNACKS	DRINKS

GROCERY LIST

TO DO LIST

NOTES:

- HOLIDAY MENU -

Date _____

STOCKED PREPPED MADE AHEAD DELEGATED DONE

BUDGET:	SPENT:	
BREAKFAST MENU		# OF GUESTS
- Protein -	- Carbs/Grains -	
- Fruit & Veggies -	- Other -	
LUNCH MENU		# OF GUESTS
- Appetizer -	- Side Dishes -	
- Main -	- Dessert -	
DINNER MENU		# OF GUESTS
- Appetizer -	- Side Dishes -	
- Main -	- Dessert -	

GROCERY LIST

TO DO LIST

SNACKS	DRINKS

NOTES:

- HOLIDAY MENU -

72

Date _____

| | STOCKED | PREPPED | MADE AHEAD | DELEGATED | DONE |

BUDGET: **SPENT:**

BREAKFAST MENU — # OF GUESTS

- Protein -

- Carbs/Grains -

- Fruit & Veggies -

- Other -

LUNCH MENU — # OF GUESTS

- Appetizer -

- Side Dishes -

- Main -

- Dessert -

DINNER MENU — # OF GUESTS

- Appetizer -

- Side Dishes -

- Main -

- Dessert -

SNACKS

DRINKS

GROCERY LIST

TO DO LIST

NOTES:

- HOLIDAY MENU -

Date _____

STOCKED PREPPED MADE AHEAD DELEGATED DONE

BUDGET:	SPENT:	
BREAKFAST MENU		# OF GUESTS
- Protein -	- Carbs/Grains -	
- Fruit & Veggies -	- Other -	
LUNCH MENU		# OF GUESTS
- Appetizer -	- Side Dishes -	
- Main -	- Dessert -	
DINNER MENU		# OF GUESTS
- Appetizer -	- Side Dishes -	
- Main -	- Dessert -	

GROCERY LIST

TO DO LIST

SNACKS	DRINKS

NOTES:

- HOLIDAY MENU -

Date _____

STOCKED | PREPPED | MADE AHEAD | DELEGATED | DONE

BUDGET:	SPENT:

BREAKFAST MENU #OF GUESTS

- Protein -	- Carbs/Grains -
- Fruit & Veggies -	- Other -

LUNCH MENU #OF GUESTS

- Appetizer -	- Side Dishes -
- Main -	- Dessert -

DINNER MENU #OF GUESTS

- Appetizer -	- Side Dishes -
- Main -	- Dessert -

GROCERY LIST

TO DO LIST

SNACKS	DRINKS

NOTES:

- HOLIDAY MENU -

Date _____

STOCKED | PREPPED | MADE AHEAD | DELEGATED | DONE

BUDGET: **SPENT:**

BREAKFAST MENU   # OF GUESTS

- Protein -

- Carbs/Grains -

- Fruit & Veggies -

- Other -

LUNCH MENU   # OF GUESTS

- Appetizer -

- Side Dishes -

- Main -

- Dessert -

DINNER MENU   # OF GUESTS

- Appetizer -

- Side Dishes -

- Main -

- Dessert -

SNACKS   DRINKS

GROCERY LIST

TO DO LIST

NOTES:

- HOLIDAY MENU -

Date _____

| STOCKED | PREPPED | MADE AHEAD | DELEGATED | DONE |

BUDGET: **SPENT:**

BREAKFAST MENU   # OF GUESTS

- Protein -

- Carbs/Grains -

- Fruit & Veggies -

- Other -

LUNCH MENU   # OF GUESTS

- Appetizer -

- Side Dishes -

- Main -

- Dessert -

DINNER MENU   # OF GUESTS

- Appetizer -

- Side Dishes -

- Main -

- Dessert -

SNACKS

DRINKS

GROCERY LIST

TO DO LIST

NOTES:

- HOLIDAY MENU -

Date _____

STOCKED PREPPED MADE AHEAD DELEGATED DONE

BUDGET:	SPENT:	
BREAKFAST MENU		# OF GUESTS
- Protein -	- Carbs/Grains -	
- Fruit & Veggies -	- Other -	
LUNCH MENU		# OF GUESTS
- Appetizer -	- Side Dishes -	
- Main -	- Dessert -	
DINNER MENU		# OF GUESTS
- Appetizer -	- Side Dishes -	
- Main -	- Dessert -	

GROCERY LIST

TO DO LIST

SNACKS	DRINKS

NOTES:

- HOLIDAY MENU -

Date: _____

STOCKED | PREPPED | MADE AHEAD | DELEGATED | DONE

BUDGET: **SPENT:**

BREAKFAST MENU   # OF GUESTS

- Protein -

- Carbs/Grains -

- Fruit & Veggies -

- Other -

LUNCH MENU   # OF GUESTS

- Appetizer -

- Side Dishes -

- Main -

- Dessert -

DINNER MENU   # OF GUESTS

- Appetizer -

- Side Dishes -

- Main -

- Dessert -

SNACKS

DRINKS

GROCERY LIST

TO DO LIST

NOTES:

- HOLIDAY RECIPES -

Dish _____

☐ Appetizer ☐ Side ☐ Main ☐ Dessert ☐ Other

| SERVINGS | PREP TIME | COOK TIME | DONE |

RECIPE

INGREDIENTS

TO DO LIST

☐
☐
☐
☐
☐
☐
☐
☐
☐
☐
☐
☐
☐
☐
☐
☐

NOTES:

RECIPE SOURCE:

- HOLIDAY RECIPES -

Dish _____

☐ Appetizer ☐ Side ☐ Main ☐ Dessert ☐ Other

SERVINGS | PREP TIME | COOK TIME | DONE

RECIPE

INGREDIENTS

TO DO LIST

NOTES:

RECIPE SOURCE:

- HOLIDAY RECIPES -

*Dish*_____

SERVINGS | PREP TIME | COOK TIME | DONE

☐ Appetizer ☐ Side ☐ Main ☐ Dessert ☐ Other

RECIPE

INGREDIENTS

TO DO LIST

☐
☐
☐
☐
☐
☐
☐
☐
☐
☐
☐
☐
☐
☐
☐
☐

NOTES:

RECIPE SOURCE:

- HOLIDAY RECIPES -

Dish _____

SERVINGS | PREP TIME | COOK TIME | DONE

☐ Appetizer ☐ Side ☐ Main ☐ Dessert ☐ Other

RECIPE

INGREDIENTS

TO DO LIST
☐
☐
☐
☐
☐
☐
☐
☐
☐
☐
☐
☐
☐
☐

NOTES:

RECIPE SOURCE:

- HOLIDAY RECIPES -

Dish _____

| SERVINGS | PREP TIME | COOK TIME | DONE |

☐ Appetizer ☐ Side ☐ Main ☐ Dessert ☐ Other

RECIPE

INGREDIENTS

TO DO LIST

☐
☐
☐
☐
☐
☐
☐
☐
☐
☐
☐
☐
☐
☐
☐

NOTES:

RECIPE SOURCE:

- HOLIDAY RECIPES -

Dish _____

SERVINGS | PREP TIME | COOK TIME | DONE

☐ Appetizer ☐ Side ☐ Main ☐ Dessert ☐ Other

RECIPE

INGREDIENTS

TO DO LIST
- ☐
- ☐
- ☐
- ☐
- ☐
- ☐
- ☐
- ☐
- ☐
- ☐
- ☐
- ☐
- ☐
- ☐
- ☐
- ☐

NOTES:

RECIPE SOURCE:

- HOLIDAY RECIPES -

Dish _____

SERVINGS PREP TIME COOK TIME DONE

☐ Appetizer ☐ Side ☐ Main ☐ Dessert ☐ Other

RECIPE

INGREDIENTS

TO DO LIST

☐
☐
☐
☐
☐
☐
☐
☐
☐
☐
☐
☐
☐
☐
☐
☐
☐

NOTES:

RECIPE SOURCE:

- HOLIDAY RECIPES -

Dish _____

SERVINGS | PREP TIME | COOK TIME | DONE

☐ Appetizer ☐ Side ☐ Main ☐ Dessert ☐ Other

RECIPE | **INGREDIENTS**

TO DO LIST

☐
☐
☐
☐
☐
☐
☐
☐
☐
☐
☐
☐
☐
☐

NOTES:

RECIPE SOURCE:

- HOLIDAY RECIPES -

Dish _____

☐ Appetizer ☐ Side ☐ Main ☐ Dessert ☐ Other

SERVINGS | PREP TIME | COOK TIME | DONE

RECIPE

INGREDIENTS

TO DO LIST

☐
☐
☐
☐
☐
☐
☐
☐
☐
☐
☐
☐
☐
☐

NOTES:

RECIPE SOURCE:

- HOLIDAY RECIPES -

Dish _____

SERVINGS | PREP TIME | COOK TIME | DONE

☐ Appetizer ☐ Side ☐ Main ☐ Dessert ☐ Other

RECIPE

INGREDIENTS

TO DO LIST
☐
☐
☐
☐
☐
☐
☐
☐
☐
☐
☐
☐
☐
☐
☐

NOTES:

RECIPE SOURCE:

- HOLIDAY RECIPES -

Dish _____

☐ Appetizer ☐ Side ☐ Main ☐ Dessert ☐ Other

SERVINGS | PREP TIME | COOK TIME | DONE

RECIPE

INGREDIENTS

TO DO LIST

☐
☐
☐
☐
☐
☐
☐
☐
☐
☐
☐
☐
☐
☐

NOTES:

RECIPE SOURCE:

- HOLIDAY RECIPES -

Dish _____

SERVINGS | PREP TIME | COOK TIME | DONE

☐ Appetizer ☐ Side ☐ Main ☐ Dessert ☐ Other

RECIPE

INGREDIENTS

TO DO LIST

☐
☐
☐
☐
☐
☐
☐
☐
☐
☐
☐
☐
☐
☐
☐

NOTES:

RECIPE SOURCE:

- HOLIDAY RECIPES -

Dish _____

☐ Appetizer ☐ Side ☐ Main ☐ Dessert ☐ Other

SERVINGS | PREP TIME | COOK TIME | DONE

RECIPE

INGREDIENTS

TO DO LIST

☐
☐
☐
☐
☐
☐
☐
☐
☐
☐
☐
☐
☐
☐
☐
☐

NOTES:

RECIPE SOURCE:

- HOLIDAY RECIPES -

Dish _____

SERVINGS | PREP TIME | COOK TIME | DONE

☐ Appetizer ☐ Side ☐ Main ☐ Dessert ☐ Other

RECIPE

INGREDIENTS

TO DO LIST

☐
☐
☐
☐
☐
☐
☐
☐
☐
☐
☐
☐
☐
☐
☐

NOTES:

RECIPE SOURCE:

- HOLIDAY RECIPES -

Dish _____

SERVINGS PREP TIME COOK TIME DONE

☐ Appetizer ☐ Side ☐ Main ☐ Dessert ☐ Other

RECIPE

INGREDIENTS

TO DO LIST

☐
☐
☐
☐
☐
☐
☐
☐
☐
☐
☐
☐
☐
☐
☐

NOTES:

RECIPE SOURCE:

- HOLIDAY RECIPES -

Dish _____

SERVINGS | PREP TIME | COOK TIME | DONE

☐ Appetizer ☐ Side ☐ Main ☐ Dessert ☐ Other

RECIPE

INGREDIENTS

TO DO LIST

NOTES:

RECIPE SOURCE:

- HOLIDAY RECIPES -

Dish _____

☐ Appetizer ☐ Side ☐ Main ☐ Dessert ☐ Other

SERVINGS PREP TIME COOK TIME DONE

RECIPE

INGREDIENTS

TO DO LIST

NOTES:

RECIPE SOURCE:

- HOLIDAY RECIPES -

Dish _____

SERVINGS | PREP TIME | COOK TIME | DONE

☐ Appetizer ☐ Side ☐ Main ☐ Dessert ☐ Other

RECIPE

INGREDIENTS

TO DO LIST

☐
☐
☐
☐
☐
☐
☐
☐
☐
☐
☐
☐
☐
☐

NOTES:

RECIPE SOURCE:

- HOLIDAY RECIPES -

Dish _____

☐ Appetizer ☐ Side ☐ Main ☐ Dessert ☐ Other

SERVINGS | PREP TIME | COOK TIME | DONE

RECIPE

INGREDIENTS

TO DO LIST

☐
☐
☐
☐
☐
☐
☐
☐
☐
☐
☐
☐
☐
☐
☐

NOTES:

RECIPE SOURCE:

- HOLIDAY RECIPES -

Dish _____

☐ Appetizer ☐ Side ☐ Main ☐ Dessert ☐ Other

SERVINGS PREP TIME COOK TIME DONE

RECIPE

INGREDIENTS

TO DO LIST

☐
☐
☐
☐
☐
☐
☐
☐
☐
☐
☐
☐
☐
☐

NOTES:

RECIPE SOURCE:

- HOLIDAY DECORATIONS INVENTORY -

Item _____ **BOX #:**

CONDITION		QUANTITY	
DESCRIPTION:			
LOCATION:	☐ For Indoor	☐ For Outdoor	☐ Other

Item _____ **BOX #:**

CONDITION		QUANTITY	
DESCRIPTION:			
LOCATION:	☐ For Indoor	☐ For Outdoor	☐ Other

Item _____ **BOX #:**

CONDITION		QUANTITY	
DESCRIPTION:			
LOCATION:	☐ For Indoor	☐ For Outdoor	☐ Other

Item _____ **BOX #:**

CONDITION		QUANTITY	
DESCRIPTION:			
LOCATION:	☐ For Indoor	☐ For Outdoor	☐ Other

- HOLIDAY DECORATIONS INVENTORY -

Item _____ **BOX #:**

CONDITION		QUANTITY	
DESCRIPTION:			
LOCATION:	☐ For Indoor	☐ For Outdoor	☐ Other

Item _____ **BOX #:**

CONDITION		QUANTITY	
DESCRIPTION:			
LOCATION:	☐ For Indoor	☐ For Outdoor	☐ Other

Item _____ **BOX #:**

CONDITION		QUANTITY	
DESCRIPTION:			
LOCATION:	☐ For Indoor	☐ For Outdoor	☐ Other

Item _____ **BOX #:**

CONDITION		QUANTITY	
DESCRIPTION:			
LOCATION:	☐ For Indoor	☐ For Outdoor	☐ Other

- MY CHRISTMAS WISHLIST -

Things I Want

Things I Need

- GIFTS I RECEIVED -

FROM	GIFT	KEEP	EXCHANGE	RETURN	RE-GIFT	THANK YOU SENT

- HOLIDAY GRATITUDE -

- FAVORITE THING -

REFLECTION

- ○ COMPLETED ALL MISSIONS
- ○ HAPPY WITH MY ACTS OF KINDNESS
- ○ REMEMBERED TO BE GRATEFUL
- ○ TOOK TIME FOR PRAYER
- ○ ENJOYED THE PROCESS

MY HOLIDAY SUCCESS RATING ☆☆☆☆☆

THANK YOU

- VISION BOARD -

My Long Term Goals

My Short Term Goals

- NEW YEAR'S RESOLUTIONS -

	GOALS	ACCOMPLISH BY	✓
1			
2			
3			
4			
5			
6			
7			
8			
9			
10			
11			
12			
13			
14			
15			
16			
17			
18			
19			
20			
21			
22			
23			
24			
25			

- CHRISTMAS & NEW YEAR'S CARD LIST -

☐ *Name* _____	**NOTES/EXTRA INFO**
📍 _____	
✉ _____	
☏ _____	

☐ *Name* _____	**NOTES/EXTRA INFO**
📍 _____	
✉ _____	
☏ _____	

☐ *Name* _____	**NOTES/EXTRA INFO**
📍 _____	
✉ _____	
☏ _____	

☐ *Name* _____	**NOTES/EXTRA INFO**
📍 _____	
✉ _____	
☏ _____	

☐ *Name* _____	**NOTES/EXTRA INFO**
📍 _____	
✉ _____	
☏ _____	

- CHRISTMAS & NEW YEAR'S CARD LIST -

☐ *Name*	NOTES/EXTRA INFO
☐ *Name*	NOTES/EXTRA INFO
☐ *Name*	NOTES/EXTRA INFO
☐ *Name*	NOTES/EXTRA INFO
☐ *Name*	NOTES/EXTRA INFO

- CHRISTMAS & NEW YEAR'S CARD LIST -

☐ *Name* _____

📍 _____
_____
_____

✉ _____
✆ _____

NOTES/EXTRA INFO

☐ *Name* _____

📍 _____
_____
_____

✉ _____
✆ _____

NOTES/EXTRA INFO

☐ *Name* _____

📍 _____
_____
_____

✉ _____
✆ _____

NOTES/EXTRA INFO

☐ *Name* _____

📍 _____
_____
_____

✉ _____
✆ _____

NOTES/EXTRA INFO

☐ *Name* _____

📍 _____
_____
_____

✉ _____
✆ _____

NOTES/EXTRA INFO

- CHRISTMAS & NEW YEAR'S CARD LIST -

☐ *Name*	NOTES/EXTRA INFO
☐ *Name*	NOTES/EXTRA INFO
☐ *Name*	NOTES/EXTRA INFO
☐ *Name*	NOTES/EXTRA INFO
☐ *Name*	NOTES/EXTRA INFO

- CHRISTMAS & NEW YEAR'S CARD LIST -

☐ *Name*	NOTES/EXTRA INFO
📍	
✉	
☎	

☐ *Name*	NOTES/EXTRA INFO
📍	
✉	
☎	

☐ *Name*	NOTES/EXTRA INFO
📍	
✉	
☎	

☐ *Name*	NOTES/EXTRA INFO
📍	
✉	
☎	

☐ *Name*	NOTES/EXTRA INFO
📍	
✉	
☎	

- CHRISTMAS & NEW YEAR'S CARD LIST -

☐ *Name*	NOTES/EXTRA INFO
☐ *Name*	NOTES/EXTRA INFO
☐ *Name*	NOTES/EXTRA INFO
☐ *Name*	NOTES/EXTRA INFO
☐ *Name*	NOTES/EXTRA INFO

- HOLIDAY NOTES -

- HOLIDAY NOTES -

HOLIDAY NOTES

- EXTRA CHECKLISTS -

EXTRA CHECKLISTS

Made in the USA
Coppell, TX
19 October 2022